Anima

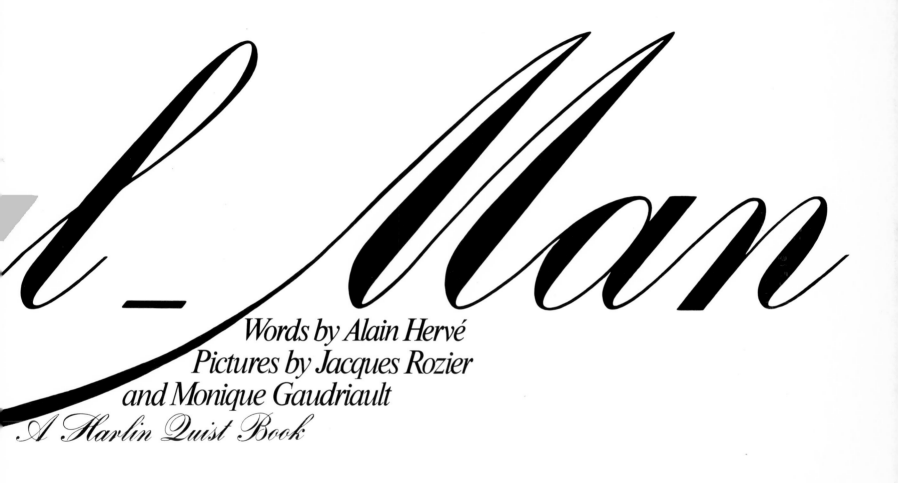

l_Man

Words by Alain Hervé
Pictures by Jacques Rozier
and Monique Gaudriault

A Harlin Quist Book

Dedicated to Anne
Published by Harlin Quist, Inc.
Library of Congress card: 76-21410
SBN: paperback: 8252-0142-X;
hardcover: 8252-0143-8
Translated by Susan Singleton

Printed in Switzerland
by Vontobel Druck A.G.
Designed by Patrick Couratin

I am the whale.
Forty million years ago,
when man did not exist,
I roamed the earth.
I went from forest floor to ocean
and man did not exist.

Now man exists
and he hunts me,
kills me, destroys me.
I am no longer safe.
No matter where I swim
I am no longer safe.

I run from man,
and he pursues me—
to the furthest reaches of the sea,
to the deepest reaches of my being.

And when the struggle ends
and I am taken,
he sings of his triumph
in his books.

Yes, man exists.
And he has crafted ships
in which to follow and pursue me.
Perilous, his travels, and far-distant—
crossing all the seven seas
till I am weakened
and succumb.

With harpoons he comes,
and knives
and rakes
and razors and shovels—
to spill my blood
and turn me
into comforts for himself.

Can you love us only
as objects, as pets, as trophies?
You trample on your bear rug
in alligator shoes
and deerskin jacket,
never caring about the lives
that died for you.

You have become a killer, man.
You wield your knives,
you aim your guns,
you jab with your hypodermic needles...
It has become
so easy to kill,
you even kill yourselves.

Man, I am the whale
and yet I speak
for all my fellow creatures
who tremble at your footsteps,
who fear your knives and guns:
the mute giraffe,
the alabaster polar bear,
the kangaroo,
the camel, the lamb, the seal.

Man, how many coats do you need?
How many rugs?
How many meals of meat?
Do we exist only for your sport
and your curious needs?
You make us your clowns.
You have even taught some of us
to carry your bombs
and to kill...

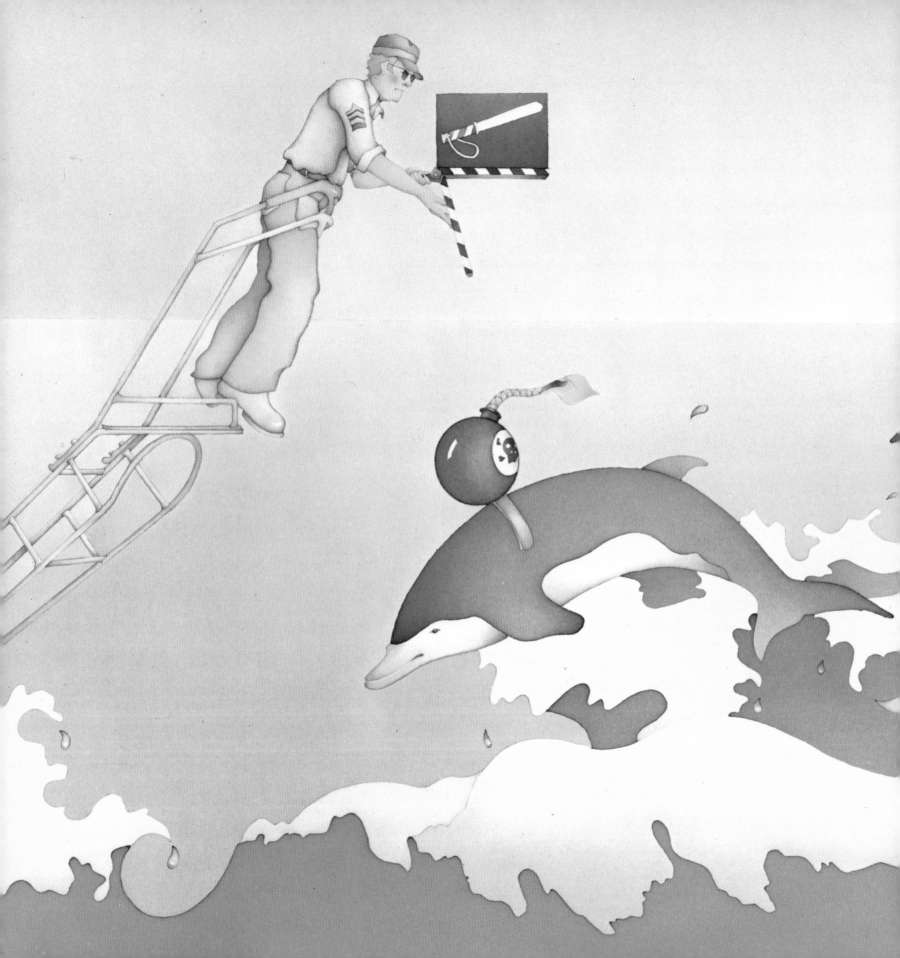

I am the whale.
When man did not exist,
I was a proud,
gargantuan
symbol of life.

Now I am
another tube of lipstick
painting someone's mouth,
a candle glowing on a dinner table,
food for household pets...

Man, there is still yet time.
Time to stop the slaughter
and the killing,
throw away the guns and knives.
I am the whale
and I know all too well
that you exist.
But I know too
that you need not exist
merely to kill all that is fragile and joyous,
all that is unique and irreplaceable and alive.

Take heed, man,
while there is time
to stop the slaughter.
Take heed.
For it is writ: an eye for an eye.
Have you forgotten?
You too are an animal, man.
And it may yet be written:
man has killed his planet,
man has killed himself,
man no longer exists...